D0579177

WHAT DOES A GOALKEEPER DO?

DO?

Paul Challen

PowerKiDS
press.

New York

Published in 2018 by The Rosen Publishing Group, Inc.
29 East 21st Street, New York, NY 10010

Developed and Produced for Rosen by BlueApple*Works* Inc.
Managing Editor for BlueApple*Works*: Melissa McClellan
Art Director: Tibor Choleva
Designer: Joshua Avramson
Photo Research: Jane Reid
Editor: Marcia Abramson

Photo Credits: Cover left J2R /Shutterstock; cover right Amy S. Myers/Dreamstime.com; title page Fotokostic/Shutterstock; TOC Olga Dmitrieva/Dreamstime.com; TOC background, background p. 8, 10, 14, 16, 20, 22, 26, 30, 32 romakoma/Shutterstock; page numbers EFKS/Shutterstock; top backgrounds p. 4, 8, 10, 14, 16, 20, 22, 26 Christian Bertrand/Shutterstock; backgrounds 6, 7, 12, 13, 18, 19, 24, 25, 28, 29 odd-add/Shutterstock; p. 4, 5 TJ Choleva; p. 5 top Daniel Kaesler/Dreamstime.com; p. 6, 10, 13, 15, 18 MaxiSports/Dreamstime.com; p. 7 Dziurek/Shutterstock; p. 8 CP DC Press/Shutterstock; p. 9 katatonia82/Shutterstock; p. 11 Iurii Osadchi/Shutterstock; p. 12 Louis Horch/Dreamstime.com; p. 14 Michael Flippo/Dreamstime.com; p. 16 Barry Austin/Thinkstock; p. 17 Ververidis Vasilis/Shutterstock; p. 19 Marcos Mesa Sam Wordley/Shutterstock; p. 20 Markus Kämmerer/Dreamstime.com; p. 21 Szirtesi/Dreamstime.com; p. 22 Mitch Gunn/Shutterstock; p. 23 Tomasz Bidermann/Shutterstock; p. 24 photo-oxser/Shutterstock; p. 25 Fotokostic/ Shutterstock; p. 25 top MediaPictures.pl/Shutterstock; p. 26 left lev radin/Shutterstock; p. 26 right Pierre-Yves Beaudouin/Wikimedia Commons/CC BY-SA 3.0; p. 27 left Stef22/Dreamstime.com; p. 27 right Fingerhut/Shutterstock; p. 27 top Cosmin Iftode/Dreamstime.com; p. 28 Randy Hjelsand/Dreamstime.com; p. 29 Jakkrit Orrasri/Shutterstock; back cover Krivosheev Vitaly

Cataloging-in-Publication Data
Names: Challen, Paul.
Title: What does a goalkeeper do? / Paul Challen.
Description: New York : PowerKids Press, 2018. | Series: Soccer smarts | Includes index.
Identifiers: ISBN 9781508154501 (pbk.) | ISBN 9781508154464 (library bound) | ISBN 9781508154389 (6 pack)
Subjects: LCSH: Soccer--Goalkeeping--Juvenile literature. | Soccer--Juvenile literature.
Classification: LCC GV943.9.G62 C53 2018 | DDC 796.334'26--dc23

Manufactured in China

CPSIA Compliance Information: Batch #BS17PK For Further Information contact: Rosen Publishing, New York, New York at 1-800-237-9932

CONTENTS

THE SOCCER TEAM

Two teams play against each other in a game of soccer. Each team has a goalkeeper, the one player who can use his or her hands when the ball is in play, and who tries to keep the other team from scoring goals. The rest of a soccer team's players can play in any other position they choose. The remaining 10 outfield players — the defenders, midfielders, and forwards — can be in any position in any number. This is known as a team's formation. Many players are able to play several positions, switching from defense to midfield to forward to help their teams.

A system of numbers is used to describe a team's formation. This system starts with the number of defenders, then midfielders, and then the forwards. A common 4-3-3 formation means that a team will play with four defenders, three midfielders, three forwards, and a goalkeeper.

Winger

Center Forward

Winger

Outside Midfielder

Center Midfielder

Outside Midfielder

Outside Back

Center Back

Center Back

Outside Back

Goalkeeper

4-3-3 Formation

THE ROLE OF THE GOALKEEPER

The goalkeeper — also known simply as the keeper — takes up a position in the goal to stop shots from the opposing team's players. It's important to remember that the keeper can actually go anywhere on the field. However, the rules of soccer say keepers can use their hands only in a marked-out area called the 18-yard box, or penalty box. If the keeper handles the ball outside the box, the referee will call a foul.

The soccer field is often called the pitch by fans and players. It has two goals on either side. End lines run behind each goal, and sidelines run along the sides. Corner flags and markings are in each of the four corners. Each goal has a 6-yard box, a penalty spot, and an 18-yard box in front of it. The center circle is right in the middle of the field.

Corner Flag

Goal

Center Circle

Corner Flag

Penalty Spot

Goal

18-yard Box

Sideline

6-yard Box

End Line

Soccer Field

5

LAST LINE OF DEFENSE

Keepers are the last line of defense on a soccer team. Because of this, they must always be alert to action on the field, especially when the opposing team has the ball near the keeper's goal. Keepers must always position themselves to be ready to stop shots, because opposing teams may decide to shoot for a goal at any time, and from almost anywhere on the pitch.

Because keepers are the only players who can touch the ball with their hands when it is in play on the field, they wear special gloves with padding that allows them to stop hard shots. Many keepers also wear special shorts, track pants, and jerseys with extra padding.

In addition to stopping shots, goalkeepers must be alert to any attackers or passes that break through their team's defense. Rather than staying in their goals for the whole game, when these situations arise, keepers must come "off their line" to rush out to stop the other team from having a chance to score. Keepers mainly use their hands to block shots, but during the fast action in a game, they often have to use their feet, legs, arms, and chest to stop shots as well. A good keeper knows how to block shots in a variety of ways, and uses fast reflexes and good body positioning to stop attackers from scoring.

*When defending a free kick, a goalkeeper has to set up and position teammates in a **wall**. This means that two or more players must stand 33 feet (10 m) back from the free kick and form a human wall together to try to block the shot. The keeper will take a position to one side of the wall. The combination of the wall and the keeper means that the whole goal is covered.*

DEFENSIVE STRATEGY

Experienced goalkeepers are always communicating with their teammates, especially the defenders. When these players work as a defensive unit within the soccer team, it can be very tough for opponents to score against them. A good keeper-defender unit can cover almost the entire goal.

Since they can see the entire game unfolding in front of them, keepers are always telling teammates how to position themselves. They must use loud, strong voices to command the area around the goal.

It is common to hear goalkeepers yelling "Keeper!" to let teammates know when they are coming to catch or collect a ball.

DEFENSE IS KEY

All good teams know that a strong defense is key to playing good soccer. Goalkeepers can combine with three, four, and sometimes five defenders to keep opponents from scoring. Many teams promote a defense-first strategy where the aim is to stop the other team from scoring, rather than just trying to score goals themselves. A strong goalkeeper is essential to this strategy.

Although defending and goalkeeping may seem a lot less glamorous than scoring goals, many coaches look to build their team "from the back." This means that they are often looking to put the strongest, most experienced players on defense and in goal.

SHOT-STOPPING SKILLS

Stopping shots is not an easy skill! Keepers need good balance, great jumping ability, and strong arms and hands for stopping shots. Even a keeper's fingers must be powerful and sturdy, because when a keeper dives to block a shot, sometimes they stop the ball with only their fingertips!

If possible, keepers want to catch shots cleanly, without dropping or fumbling the ball. But because many shots come in too fast or at awkward angles, keepers often have to do their best just to block them.

Catching shots cleanly prevents any rebounds from dropping at the feet of incoming attackers who would be only too happy to kick them into the goal.

COVERING THE GOAL

Keepers need to know how to position themselves in the goal before an opponent shoots so that they have the best chance to stop the shot. The **starting position** on every shot is crucial because it gives a keeper a head start in reacting. To have a good starting position, keepers need to know where shots can come from, and the agility and quick reflexes to react.

Part of effective shot stopping involves "cutting down the angle." This means moving ahead of the goal line to give an opponent less of an angle to shoot on goal.

When a keeper cuts down a shooter's angle, the attacking player has less space to aim for between the keeper and the goal.

БОЙКО
71

DCH

DISTRIBUTION

When keepers have made a save, they need to be skilled at **distributing** the ball to teammates. This can be done through long or short kicks from the ground, or as **drop kicks** from the keeper's hands. It's also important to be able to make long or short throws and to roll the ball along the ground. Good distribution is key to a team's overall play, because it helps to keep possession of the ball.

There is little point in a keeper making a great save only to give the ball away to the opponents with a wild kick or poor throw.

THROWING

A goalkeeper's throws are different from those in other sports such as football or baseball. Instead of snapping at the elbow to release the ball as is common in these sports, keepers use a locked-elbow style that makes a ball easier to control when it comes to a teammate.

Being able to roll a ball accurately to a teammate is also a very important goalkeeping skill. Once again, rolling the ball along the ground makes it very easy for a teammate to bring the ball under control before they dribble or pass it.

Soccer keepers use an underhanded motion to roll a ball, very similar to the one used in bowling.

CATCHING

Being able to catch a ball cleanly, without fumbling or "spilling" it, is one of the most important skills a goalkeeper can have. To catch a ball cleanly, the keeper must place the thumbs behind the ball to give extra backing to the fingers and palms. Keepers must also concentrate and watch a ball all the way into their gloves. Spilling needs to be avoided so offensive players do not have a chance to pick up rebounds.

The "W" position is a popular and effective way that soccer goalkeepers use to catch a ball cleanly. By spreading the palms out with thumbs touching behind the ball, the hands form a "W" pattern — one that is very sturdy and makes it hard for balls to get through.

PARRYING

Sometimes when a shot is coming in too fast it is safer for a keeper not to catch the ball but to **parry** it away. Blazing fast shots can often travel right through the fingers and palms, so parrying can be a safer shot-stopping try. To parry a ball, keepers must make two fists, and place the hands right together to make contact with both. This also requires locked elbows so the ball hits a firm, solid surface and bounces away to safety.

Keepers and defenders must be alert for rebounds in situations when the keeper does not save the ball cleanly. When there is a scramble near the goal after this happens, keepers will often shout "Away!" to tell their teammates that the safest action is to kick the ball away rather than trying to pass it.

DEALING WITH CROSSES

Goalkeepers must also know how to deal with **crosses** in the air. To intercept a cross, keepers must square their body to face the crossing player and must leap high to catch the ball before an opponent can head it towards goal.

Sometimes keepers cannot catch a cross cleanly, so they must punch the ball with a closed fist to knock it away. Keepers must also communicate with defenders to let them know when they are coming to "collect," or catch, a cross.

Keepers must jump and extend their arms high in the air to grab the ball. This allows them to reach balls much higher in the air than players who cannot use their hands.

DID YOU KNOW?

In a penalty kick, keepers try to stop a shot from the penalty spot. It's just the shooter against the keeper, one on one. The rules of soccer say the keeper must be on their goal line when the penalty is kicked, although a keeper can bounce up and down and go back and forth along the line. Experienced keepers will try to guess which way a shooter will go with a shot, and dive in that direction to save it.

DEFENDING CORNERS

When the opposing team is taking a corner kick, keepers also have an important job. The skills in stopping a corner kick are similar to dealing with crosses — catching, punching, and good positioning are all important. It can be very crowded in the goal area during corner kicks, so keepers need to be alert and aggressive to get any balls that come their way.

Sometimes keepers cannot catch or punch the ball cleanly and simply have to slap an aerial ball to safety, as an absolute emergency measure. Soccer commentators sometimes call this "flapping" at the ball.

17

BODY BACKUP

When stopping shots with the hands, it is crucial that a keeper get some other body part like a leg, the stomach, or the chest behind the ball. This is because if the keeper somehow allows the ball through the hands it will hit one of these other body parts and not end up in the net.

Keepers use a common technique to stop rolling shots from going between their legs and into the goal. The keeper will drop to one knee, forming a barrier with the leg behind their hands. This way, even if the keeper's hands somehow fumble the ball, the back leg will stop it.

After the save is made, the soccer ball should be securely held in front of the goalkeeper.

GETTING BIG

When facing a shooter in a one-on-one situation, coaches tell goalkeepers to "get big" by taking up as much space as possible and reducing the space a shooter has to aim at. Keepers do this by extending their arms and spreading their legs wide to take away the space. When shooters face a "big" keeper, especially under pressure by a defender, they may often rush the shot, or miss the goal entirely. This is why it is very important for keepers not to turn sideways or turn their back at a shooter.

Along with getting big, smart keepers closely watch the ball and the body language of the opponent. If necessary, they will get off the line and run at their opponent.

OUTFIELD SKILLS

At higher levels of soccer, teams rely on their keeper to be much more than a shot-stopper. They must have the same good foot skills as an outfield player so they can receive and send paces. This includes accurate control with both feet, the ability to make short and long passes, and sometimes even dribbling to evade oncoming attackers.

According to the rules of soccer, keepers cannot use their hands to control a pass kicked intentionally to them from a teammate. Keepers can use the hands to control a headed pass to them, however, and are allowed to handle balls that come accidentally back to them from the feet of teammates.

It's rare for a keeper to score a goal, but José Luis Chilavert of Paraguay scored 67 of them in his pro career with several teams. Chilavert also was the keeper of Paraguay's national team from 1989 to 2003 and its captain at the World Cup in 1998 and 2002. He often was called upon to take penalty kicks and free kicks because he was such an accurate and powerful kicker. He is the only known keeper to have scored three goals (a hat trick) in a one game. Known as "The Bulldog," he was also an expert shot-stopper.

USING YOUR HEAD

Keepers often also must head the ball, especially when they have come out of their area to clear a long ball in the air. Because they cannot touch the ball with their hands outside their own penalty area, an acrobatic diving header is often the best way of getting the ball to safety.

Keepers often must head the ball, especially when they have come out of their area to clear a long ball in the air. Because they cannot touch the ball with their hands outside their own penalty area, an acrobatic diving header is often the best way of getting the ball to safety.

THE SWEEPER KEEPER

As the game of soccer has changed over the years, one of the biggest differences has been the much more active role that goalkeepers play in games. Today, many teams actually use their goalkeeper as an extra defender, positioned behind the back line to sweep up any balls that go past the last line of players.

Known as the **sweeper keeper**, this player must have the skills and confidence to leave the goal at the right time, but must also know when to stay back and stop shots.

Sweeper keepers have high "soccer IQs" and know how to "read" the game brilliantly. They are able to play with their feet and head with equal skill to any defender. In the pro game, many of these sweeper keepers run almost as far as their defensive teammates!

THE OFFSIDE TRAP

The rules of soccer say that an attacking player cannot be offside behind the last defender (not including the keeper) when a pass is played forward in their attacking half of the field. To try to put opposing forwards offside, defenders will often push up past the attacker. Goalkeepers are often responsible for organizing the defense in this "offside trap" but have to be careful. If a ball is played over or through the trap, the keeper has to know when to rush out of the goal to claim or clear it.

Knowing when to dash off the goal line is key for any keeper. They must communicate with their defenders to let them know when they are coming to claim a ball.

THE ROLE OF A HEAD COACH

Head coaches set the team's formation, pick which players will be in the team's starting 11, and decide which players will be the substitutes for each game. Head coaches are responsible for the major coaching decisions during a game and are often active on the sidelines, yelling instructions to players.

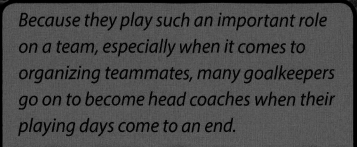

Because they play such an important role on a team, especially when it comes to organizing teammates, many goalkeepers go on to become head coaches when their playing days come to an end.

Professional head coaches must stay in one spot during a game. This is called the technical area and is located along the sideline, close to a team's bench. The only time a head coach can leave this area is to attend to a player with an injury. However, in the professional game, specially trained assistants called "physios" usually help players who have been injured during play.

With the help of their assistant coaches, head coaches also set up and run training sessions. They help players build their individual skills and work on their strength and fitness. Head coaches work on team tactics, and it's common for them to watch videos of opposing teams before games to notice their strengths and weaknesses.

The steady nerves and calm decision-making abilities of many keepers also mean they make excellent coaches.

THE BEST KEEPERS

All-time great keepers include Hope Solo of the United States, who played a key role in her country's win at the 2015 World Cup. Russian superstar Lev Yashin was called the "Black Spider" because of his all-black **kit** and because he saved shots so well it sometimes seemed he had eight arms and legs! Among the many accomplishments of retired German keeper Nadine Angerer was her unbelievable record set at the 2007 World Cup tournament. Angerer did not allow a single goal in all six games played by Germany on their way to becoming world champions.

American Nick Rimando (left) may be one of the smallest keepers in pro soccer, but his incredible agility and shot-stopping skill make him one of the best in Major League Soccer (MLS) and a member of the US Men's National Team. Sarah Bouhaddi of France (right) is a standout for her country's national team and for the Olympique Lyonais team in the French women's pro league.

Many soccer fans consider Gianluigi Buffon of the Italian national team and the Juventus club team to be one of the greatest soccer keepers of all time.

Buffon started playing as a keeper when he was a teenager. He led the Azzurri, which is the Italian national team's nickname, to victory at the 2006 World Cup. In 2016, he was still going strong at the age of 38. Buffon combines astonishing shot-stopping skills with great distribution and leadership on the pitch where he serves as Italy's captain.

Chile's Claudio Bravo helped his country win back-to-back Copa America titles in 2015 and 2016, and plays for English giants Manchester City. American Tim Howard had a long career in the English Premier League, and at the 2014 World Cup set an all-time single game record for the tournament with an incredible 14 saves in one game.

Manuel Neuer of Germany and Bayern Munich (right) is one of the best. He helped his team win the 2014 World Cup and has completely revolutionized the game with his sweeper keeper skills. Spaniard David De Gea (left) has an array of unusual but highly effective shot-stopping techniques which he uses to help his country and Manchester United in the English Premier League.

BE A GOOD SPORT

Soccer is called "the beautiful game," and one of the main reasons for this nickname is that its players, fans, officials, and coaches have traditionally followed the principles of sportsmanship and fair play. For example, it's common for players to kick the ball out of bounds when an opponent is hurt or injured so they can receive treatment. Soccer players often help fallen opponents up off the pitch, and strong teams usually refuse to run up a big score against weaker teams.

Young players should remember that it never hurts to give a big thanks to the people who help and support them in developing their skills and building their love of the game.

RESPECTING THE REFEREES

Referees to do the best job they can, but because they are human, they do make mistakes. Players, parents, and coaches must always show respect for the refs — no matter the level of play. Yelling at the refs or arguing calls is poor sportsmanship, and it's not a good way to help a team.

RESPECT

It's a general rule in soccer that teams who show respect for their opponents are likely to get that respect back. Players should always try to give 100 percent of their effort in games, but going all-out to win should never be more important than showing respect for the game, for teammates, and for opponents. Trying to bend the rules or cheat spoils the game for everyone.

Even in the most high-pressure games, like the World Cup, fair play is very important to fans and players alike.

29

GLOSSARY

clean sheet A game in which a goalkeeper does not allow any goals to be scored by the opposition.

crosses Aerial passes, usually delivered from the wing with the intention of being headed on goal.

distributing The act of passing, either by throwing, rolling, or kicking the ball from a keeper to a teammate.

drop kick A long clearance kick by a goalkeeper in which the ball is dropped from the hands to the kicking foot and kicked powerfully.

kit The standard equipment and clothing worn by players during a soccer game.

parry To knock away a shot in order to save it.

starting position The first stage of shot-stopping, in which a goalkeeper prepares to dive to stop a shot.

sweeper keeper A goalkeeper who also plays as last defender, coming well out of goal to sweep up any balls that get past the last line of defense.

wall A combination of two or more defensive players who set up together to try to block a free kick.

FOR MORE INFORMATION

FURTHER READING

Howard, Tim. *The Keeper: The Unguarded Story of Tim Howard*. HarperCollins, 2014.

Nixon, James. *Defending and Goaltending*. Smart Apple Media, 2012.

Solo, Hope. *Hope Solo: My Story Young Readers' Edition*. HarperCollins, 2013.

WEBSITES

Due to the changing nature of Internet links, PowerKids Press has developed an online list of websites related to the subject of this book. This site is updated regularly. Please use this link to access the list:

www.powerkidslinks.com/ss/goalkeeper

INDEX